Gram's
GIFT

AuthorHouse™
1663 Liberty Drive
Bloomington, IN 47403
www.authorhouse.com
Phone: 1 (800) 839-8640

Because of the dynamic nature of the Internet, any web addresses or
links contained in this book may have changed since publication and
may no longer be valid. The views expressed in this work are solely those
of the author and do not necessarily reflect the views of the publisher,
and the publisher hereby disclaims any responsibility for them.

This book is printed on acid-free paper.

ISBN: 978-1-7283-6280-9 (sc)
ISBN: 978-1-7283-6281-6 (e)
ISBN: 978-1-7283-6282-3 (hc)

Library of Congress Control Number: 2020909549

Print information available on the last page.

Published by AuthorHouse 07/21/2020

authorHOUSE®

Gram's GIFT

JOYCE MOSLEY

GRAM'S GIFT

For over sixty-five years, my mother's side of the family, the Millers, have gathered in Philadelphia, Pennsylvania, the first weekend in July to attend our family reunion. Besides Christmas, this is my favorite time of the year because I get to hang out with my out-of-state cousins. My aunts and their families always camp out at my house for the long weekend. All us kids look forward to spending this time together. Gram always arrives Thursday morning so she and Mom can spend the day cooking family dishes passed down from generation to generation, like Mexican chili with canned corn. Each evening, we sit around the dinner table, sharing family jokes, eating, and listening to Gram's stories. Gram writes children's books, so she has the very best stories. But this year was different.

After dinner, Gram stood up and said, "I want all you children to follow me into the living room. It is time you learned about our family history. You should know the contributions made by your ancestors. Our family has lived on this land since before the Revolutionary War and before America was a nation. We have a long and distinguished history, and I want you to know what an awesome family you were born into."

So, my sisters, my brother, and all my cousins followed Gram into the living room to begin our family history lesson. Gram sat in the high-backed chair and got comfortable, while all of us kids sat on the floor in front of her chair, waiting to hear Gram's history lesson.

Cyrus Bustill

Gram said, "I want to start with Cyrus Bustill, my sixth great grandfather. He was born on February 2, 1732, in Burlington, New Jersey. He was born enslaved. Cyrus and his mother, Parthenia, were the property of Samuel Bustill, Sr., Cyrus' grandfather. Cyrus was a mulatto, a mixed-race person, with a white father and an African mother."

Jordan asked, "Why did Cyrus' grandfather own him? People should not be the property of other people."

Gram explained that slavery was an ugly period in the history of this country. For hundreds of years, Africans were brought to this country and sold into slavery. Africans came to this country under horrible conditions, were sold to other people, and had no human rights. Children born to enslaved women were born into slavery and considered the property of the person who owned their mother. Since Cyrus' mother was the property of his grandfather, Samuel Bustill, Sr., Cyrus was also the property of his grandfather. Cyrus' grandfather and his father, Samuel Bustill, Jr., were highly-regarded leaders in their Burlington, New Jersey community. Samuel Bustill Sr. and his son were appointed to several government offices, including being a judge and served New Jersey with integrity, but they were also slave owners. Cyrus was treated as an enslaved child owned by the Bustill family, not as a son.

Shane asked, "What is the difference between being a slave and being enslaved?"

Gram told us that a slave is a person who is the legal property of another person. Africans brought to this land did not want to be slaves—they were forced into slavery. They were enslaved. Today, we use the term *enslaved* to show that Africans had no control over their lives. Africans were not slaves when they were captured in Africa. They were doctors, teachers, fishermen, builders, business people, and parents. They were enslaved when they arrived in slaveholding countries.

Miles waved his hand and said, "Gram, do you know that my middle name is Cyrus?"

Gram nodded her head and said, "You are a lucky boy. Many men in our family are named after the first Cyrus. My great-grandfather, my grandfather, two of my uncles, several cousins, and you were all named Cyrus. In our family, Cyrus is the name of a man of whom we are very proud, and we have kept the name in our family over the generations."

"Let me continue with our family history lesson," Gram said, as she sat back in her chair.

Gram told us that while many enslaved children were taken from their families and sold away from the people who loved them, Cyrus lived on his grandfather's land with his mother, grandmother, sister, and other enslaved Africans—all the property of the Bustill family. Cyrus' mother was a kind, caring woman who showed him a lot of love, but she was very strict with him, so he would learn the life lessons needed to protect him as an enslaved child. Children that broke these rules were often beaten or sold away from their family. Therefore, it was important that Cyrus knew what was expected of him and how to act around white people. For example, children who talked back to adults could be beaten or worse.

She also said that as a member of the Bustill slave household, Cyrus' mother's job was to clean, cook, and serve their guests. As a toddler, Cyrus was allowed to play in the corner of the room while his mother completed her daily chores. Enslaved children were not allowed to attend school; instead, when Cyrus was school age, he was assigned small cleaning tasks. One day while he swept the dining room floor, he heard his father and his friends talking in the next room. His father, a Judge for Colonial New Jersey, and Benjamin Franklin from Philadelphia were discussing the first printing of paper money in New Jersey. Cyrus did not understand everything the men were talking about, but he knew Benjamin Franklin was a friend of his father's, and these men were assigned a significant job for the people of New Jersey.

Gram said, "I know this because Benjamin Franklin wrote about working with Samuel Bustill in his autobiography."

Kevin told Gram he couldn't wait to tell his teacher that a member of our family worked with Benjamin Franklin.

Gram explained that the Bustill family were Quakers, members of the Society of Friends. In colonial days, Quakers were known by how they talked, dressed, and practiced their religion. Many Quakers were abolitionists, which means they were against slavery, and many helped run-away slaves on their journey to freedom. Quakers established rules against their members owning slaves. When Samuel Bustill, Sr. was encouraged by his fellow Quakers to free his slaves, he did not.

Gram said, "I'd like to think it was because some of his slaves were his family. I believe he wanted to ensure his slaves stayed under his protection.

When Cyrus was eight years old, his father died, and two years later, his grandfather died. The death of his grandfather changed Cyrus' life forever. In his grandfather's will, he left instructions for his wife to make arrangements for Cyrus' future. Instead, she sold him to Judge John Allen. So, at the age of ten, Cyrus was forced to move away from his mother, grandmother, and other members of his family. He was sent to live on his new owner's land. He was now the property of Judge Allen and served the Allen family until he was an adult. Judge Allen often told Cyrus that as a reward for being a good worker, he would be his last slave owner. He would emancipate Cyrus."

Gram told us, "*Emancipated* meant the Judge would grant Cyrus his freedom. Cyrus would no longer be someone's property. He would have control over his life. Cyrus would decide where to go, what work to do, and where to live. Unfortunately, Judge Allen died before setting Cyrus free. Mrs. Allen would have freed him, but her son wanted the money he would receive from selling Cyrus."

Despite the fact that Quakers banned their members from purchasing or owning slaves, Cyrus approached Thomas Pryor, a Quaker, to asked him to purchase him and allow Cyrus to work for seven years. At the end of the seven years, Cyrus would be emancipated. He would be freed. Thomas Pryor, Judge Allen's nephew, watched Cyrus grow up from the age of ten and knew him to be a good man. So, he agreed to purchase Cyrus. At age thirty, Cyrus became the property of Thomas Pryor. Seven years later, Cyrus was no longer someone's property. He was a free man.

Troi said, "Cyrus is no longer enslaved. Cyrus is free." All of us kids clapped our hands and high-fived each other. We were so happy.

Gram said that Quaker records indicate that Thomas Pryor granted Cyrus his freedom in 1769, making him one of the one hundred four enslaved Negroes manumitted at the Burlington Quarterly Meeting of Friends. Gram said that *manumitted* means the freeing of an enslaved person. Back then, people of African descent were referred to as *Negroes* or *colored*.

Jeremiah said, "Wow, there are a lot of words for freedom, like manumitted and emancipated. The important thing is that Cyrus was free."

Gram proudly said, "During the time Cyrus was owned by Thomas Pryor, he learned to bake. With extra money he earned from selling bread, Cyrus hired a boy to teach him to read and write. He had reading, and writing lessons as the bread was baking and practiced his reading by candlelight at night. Even though he was an adult, it was important for him to learn to read and write. He wanted to be educated so that, when he had children, he could educate them. Education has always been important in our family, and it was very important to Cyrus."

Jasmine said, "Our parents are always encouraging us to learn more, to read more, and to study harder. Now, I know why."

Gram told us that Cyrus' good friend, Caesar Morrey, introduced Cyrus to his sister, Elizabeth, a free woman living in Philadelphia. Like Cyrus, Elizabeth lived a Quaker lifestyle in practice and dress. They were married in Philadelphia at Christ Church on August 6, 1773.

With a great deal of pride, Gram said, "For many years, Cyrus successfully operated a bakery in Burlington, New Jersey. During the Revolutionary War, he baked bread for the Continental troops, and he was one of the bakers recruited to supply bread to troops camped at Valley Forge, Pennsylvania. According to our family history, George Washington gave Cyrus a silver dollar for his dedication to providing bread to his starving soldiers. Passed down from generation to generation in our family is an affidavit certifying that Cyrus was commissioned to bake bread by the Quartermaster Department of the Continental Army. This was a huge honor for a man who was born enslaved. Let me read this document to you."

I hereby certify that Cyrus Bustill has been employed in the baking of all the flour used at the port of Burlington and that he has behaved himself as a faithful, honest man and has given satisfaction such as should recommend him to every good inhabitant.

Given under my hand at Burlington, May 1, 1782.

(Signed)

THOMAS FALCOMER

Contractor for supplying troops at the above-mentioned port."

Adrian said, "That paper has been in our family for a very long time."

Gram explained that because Cyrus baked and delivered bread to the troops in Valley Forge the winter of 1777, she is a member of the Daughters of the American Revolution (DAR). The DAR is an organization of women who are direct descendants of a person who contributed to this country's fight for independence from England. The certificate from Thomas Falcomer was one of the documents used to prove Cyrus' contribution to the Revolutionary War.

We listened as Gram told us one of her favorite stories about Cyrus. She said, "One day, Cyrus was riding his horse along a dirt road when he came upon a local judge, who was a good customer of his bakery, riding in his buggy on the same road. The judge's buggy was moving slowly enough to limit the amount of dust his horse and buggy kicked up on him, but moving fast enough so that Cyrus was riding in his dust cloud. It was the custom of the times that Cyrus, being of lower social status, would slow down, stay behind the judge and ride in the dust kicked up by the judge's horse. Cyrus feeling equal in status to any man, sped up and passed the judge so that he, the judge, was now riding in the dust created by Cyrus' horse. The judge shouted, "Cyrus, I will no longer buy any bread from your bakery." Cyrus shouted back, "So be it, Judge," and rode off down the road. Later, the judge, missing Cyrus' delicious baked goods, returned to shopping at his bakery.

Gram continued by saying, "After the Revolutionary War, Cyrus moved his family to Philadelphia, where he operated a bakery at 210 Arch Street, and he became a leader in the black community. In 1787, he was one of the founders of Philadelphia's Free African Society. This organization established schools for free children, cared for the poor, and protected run-away slaves. The society supported the needs of enslaved and free Africans. Even though Cyrus followed the religious practices of Quakers, he financially supported several black churches, including the African Episcopal Church of St. Thomas and the First African Presbyterian Church, both churches located in South Philadelphia."

Gram said, "Let me tell you what kind of a man Cyrus was. Cyrus' mother, Parthenia, was never freed. She was the property of the Bustill family her entire life. When she was old and no longer able to perform her duties as an enslaved woman in the Bustill household, her devoted son went to Burlington, New Jersey (a long way by horse and buggy), to bring his elderly mother to live with him. Cyrus and the family lovingly cared for Parthenia until she died in 1790." Gram proudly said, "I have a copy of a letter written by Cyrus to the man who owned his mother. Cyrus' letter informs him that Parthenia was ill, and he should come soon if he wanted to see her before she passed. Imagine having a copy of a letter written in 1790. This letter is over two hundred years old."

Jasmine said, "That is amazing!"

With a lot of pride in her voice Gram said, "In 1803, after Cyrus retired from operating his bakery, he started a school in his house for colored youth. Cyrus wrote that all children should have the opportunity to be educated. He operated his school until his death in 1806. I believe his school merged with another

Quaker-operated school after his death. Cyrus dedicated his life to improving the conditions of the people in his community and helping those still enslaved."

Gram told us that when Cyrus died two unusual things happened: (1) the white community published his obituary, a notice of a person's death printed in the newspaper, and (2) the Society of Friends conducted his funeral service, so he was buried as a Quaker even though he was never accepted for membership. Family records state that Cyrus was buried in our family's cemetery in Glenside, Pennsylvania. According to current maps, the cemetery lot is now under a county street that was widened many years after Cyrus died.

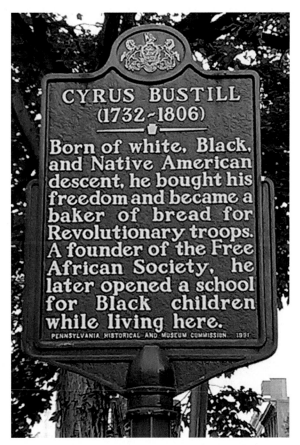

(used with permission of the Pennsylvania Historical and Museum Commission)

On April 29, 2000, the Pennsylvania Historical and Museum Commission dedicated a state historical marker on the site of Cyrus' bakery at 210 Arch Street.

Elizabeth Morrey Bustill

Gram said, "Now that you know about Cyrus, let's talk about Elizabeth Morrey Bustill, his wife. She was born free in 1742, the daughter of Richard Morrey and Cremona Satterthwaite, a servant in the Morrey household. Elizabeth's grandfather, Humphrey Morrey, freed Cremona before Elizabeth was born. Therefore, since Cremona was a free woman, her five children were born free. The Morrey children were also mixed-race, with a white father and a mother with African and Native American roots."

Elizabeth's grandfather, Humphrey Morrey, arrived in the colonies in the 1670s, landing in Oyster Bay, NY. He first came to Philadelphia in 1683. He purchased land from his friend, William Penn, both in Philadelphia and outside the city limits in what is now Cheltenham Township. The Morrey family was among the first fifteen families to live in the township. In 1685, and then again in 1687, Humphrey Morrey was appointed Justice of the Peace, and in 1690 he was appointed to the colonial legislative assembly. When Philadelphia was incorporated as a city in 1691, Humphrey was appointed Mayor by William Penn for a ten-year term. Children, this means you are related to the first Mayor of the city we live in."

Jeremiah said, "Wow, our family has a very long history in our hometown."

Gram explained, "Elizabeth's parents had five children with Elizabeth being their middle child. Although it was against the law for her parents to marry, they lived as husband and wife, and Cremona took "Morrey" as her last name like all wives did back then."

Alex shouted out, "That law was not fair! If we lived back then, my parents couldn't get married. I don't like that law."

Gram said, "Richard and Cremona could not legally marry, but to ensure Cremona and their children were taken care of after his death, Richard arranged for a Quaker neighbor to supervise the transfer of one hundred ninety-eight acres of land to Cremona upon his death. Today located on the land, is a house built by Cousin Hiram Montier in 1772 and a portion of Arcadia University's campus.

Tomorrow, while we are all in town for the family reunion, we are going to visit our family land. I look forward to walking around the college campus to show you the land our ancestors lived on over three hundred forty years ago. While we are talking about cousin Hiram Montier, let me tell you something special about our Morrey cousin. Wedding portraits of Hiram Montier and his bride, Elizabeth Brown Montier, are currently on display at the Philadelphia Museum of Art. They are the only known wedding portraits of an African-American couple painted during that period. Our family loaned the portraits to the museum so others can share the beauty of the paintings."

Wedding portraits of Hiram Montier and Elizbeth Brown Montier painted by Franklin R Street in 1841.

Jordan said. "Mom took us to see the portraits last month. We felt like superstars standing in front of portraits of our family members displayed in a museum."

Gram said, "Like Cyrus, Elizabeth lived a Quaker lifestyle, and together, they reared their eight children as Quakers. Their children were educated and grew up to be community leaders and business owners in early Philadelphia. Elizabeth was very active in the religious and social life of her community. For example, during the Yellow Fever epidemic in Philadelphia, she cared for the sick and dying and raised funds to feed orphans. She was a smart businesswoman. After Cyrus' death, she operated her own business. She died in 1827 at the age of eighty-five."

Marquis said, "We are an African-American family, but we have white people as part of our family. How can that be?"

Gram answered that during slavery, many enslaved women had children by white slave owners, overseers, or other men who had power over them. Also, as in our family, people with European, Native American, and African roots fell in love and had children. Like many families in America who can trace their roots to slavery, we are a mixed-race family. In the past, mixed-race people were called "mulattos." When you look at family photos, our skin coloring ranges from very pale to dark brown. Today, there are African-American Bustills and white Bustills as well as African-American and white Morreys."

Just as Gram was about to tell us about the eight Bustill children, Mom said, "Okay, kids, it is time for bed, so you will have to continue your family history lesson tomorrow." We asked if we could have five more minutes. "Please, Mom, just five more minutes." But Mom said, "No," so off to bed we went. As I lay in my bed, I feel sad thinking I am the same age as Cyrus when he was sold away from his family. I can't wait for the morning, so I can learn more about my family. I fell asleep thinking about what it must be like to be someone's property.

BUSTILL FAMILY TREE

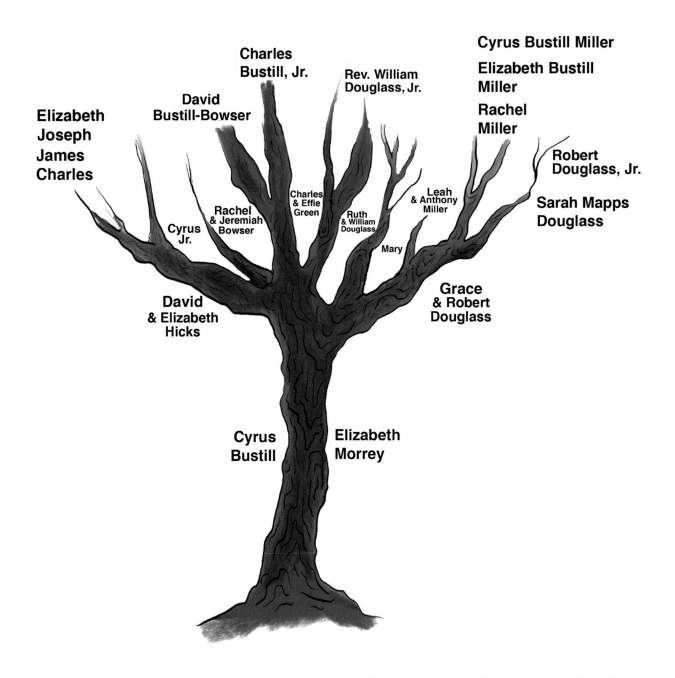

Cyrus Bustill Miller

Elizabeth Bustill
Miller

Rachel
Miller

Robert
Douglass, Jr.

Sarah Mapps
Douglass

Charles
Bustill, Jr.

Rev. William
Douglass, Jr.

David
Bustill-Bowser

Elizabeth
Joseph
James
Charles

Charles
& Effie
Green

Leah
& Anthony
Miller

Rachel
& Jeremiah
Bowser

Ruth
& William
Douglass

Cyrus
Jr.

Mary

Grace
& Robert
Douglass

David
& Elizabeth
Hicks

Cyrus
Bustill

Elizabeth
Morrey

The Bustill Children

I woke up the next morning and ran downstairs. Gram was sitting at the kitchen table drinking her coffee. I asked her to continue the family history lesson, but she said that I had to wait until all the children were up and dressed. I ran back upstairs and rushed everyone to get dressed and back downstairs to devour breakfast. I wanted to know more about my family. I wanted to know about the Bustill children. When everyone finished breakfast and the dishes were cleared from the table, Gram said, "Where do I start?"

Amari said, "You were going to tell us about the Bustill children when Mom said it was bedtime."

Gram put her coffee cup down on the kitchen table and started day two of our family history lesson.

Gram said, "There were eight Bustill children—Cyrus, Jr., Ruth, Mary, Leah, Charles, Rachel, David, and Grace. They were educated and many, following in their parents' footsteps, became business owners. Cyrus Bustill's legacy and influence in his community was carried on by his children. I am still researching the lives of the children. It appears that Cyrus Jr. and Mary may have died young as I can only find limited information on their lives. So, let me tell you what I have learned about the other Bustill children.

Ruth Bustill

Ruth Bustill married William Douglass, Sr. of Bristol, Pennsylvania. Their daughter, Anna, was a teacher in a private school for children of color in Burlington, New Jersey, for many years. Their son, the Rev. William Douglass, Jr., was the second pastor of the African Episcopal Church of St. Thomas. As I mentioned yesterday, this has been our family church since the church opened its doors in 1792. Rev. William Douglass published a book about the history of the church entitled *The Annals of the First African Church in the United States of America.*

Rachel Bustill

Rachel Bustill married Jeremiah Bowser, a steward working on ships that sailed from Liverpool, England to Philadelphia. A steward's job is similar to a hotel maid's job except stewards work on ships at sea. One afternoon while walking in his Philadelphia neighborhood, Jeremiah Bowser was mistaken for a run-away slave and arrested. Slave Catchers, people paid to hunt down and return run-away slaves to their owners, were going to take him south to be enslaved. Fortunately, a group of Quaker men who knew him to be a free man stepped in and prevented the Slave Catchers from selling Jeremiah into slavery.

Jeremiah and Rachel's son, David Bustill Bowser, was an ornamental artist and a portrait painter who also designed and painted hats for volunteer fire companies.

Volunteer Fire Company Hat painted by David Bustill Bowser

David attended a private school for colored children run by his cousin, Sarah Mapps Douglass, and studied art with Sarah's older brother, Robert Douglass, Jr. During the Civil War, David Bustill Bowser was commissioned to paint eleven regiment flags for the United States Colored Troops (USCT). Regiment flags were important back then because the flags let the soldiers know the location of their unit on the battlefield.

"We will Prove Ourselves Men"
1864 battle flag, 127ᵗʰ Regiment U.S. Colored Troops by David Bustill Bowser

I am sad to say that there is only one flag left, which is currently hanging in the Atlanta History Center in Atlanta, Georgia. This regimental flag depicts an African-American soldier standing next to Columbia, an early America representation of lady liberty, holding a flag."

Shane asked, "Will you take us to see the last flag?"

Gram said, "Great idea! I can look into planning a trip this fall."

Gram continued by saying, "David Bustill Bowser painted a portrait of President Abraham Lincoln from a photograph. He also painted a portrait of abolitionist John Brown while he was in Philadelphia working for the Underground Railroad and raising money for his raid on Harpers Ferry. John Brown's portrait was painted while he was a guest in David Bustill Bowser's house, which was also a stop on the Underground Railroad."

***Portrait of abolitionist, John Brown painted by David Bustill
Bowser in his house in Philadelphia in 1860***

Gram said, "Before we move on, let me quickly tell you about David's children. David Bustill Bowser was the father of Raphael Bowser and Ida Elizabeth Bowser. Raphael followed in his father's footsteps and worked as an artist. His sister, Ida, played the violin and taught music. She received a Certificate of Proficiency in Music from the University of Pennsylvania in June of 1890, becoming the first

African-American woman to graduate from the University of Pennsylvania. Ida married John Cornelius Asbury, a politician, businessman, successful attorney, and a member of the Pennsylvania State Assembly among other organizations.

AJ said, "Gram, I like to draw and paint. I want to be an artist when I grow up." Jeremiah and Amri both said they also want to be artists. Gram told us, many family members are talented artists and musicians. These talents were passed down generation to generation.

Just then, Mom interrupted to announce we were missing out on a beautiful summer day, and we should go outside to enjoy the day. She told us that we could continue our family history lesson after dinner.

After Dinner

All us kids agreed that we would eat dinner as fast as we can so we could meet Gram in the living room for our next lesson. We ate quickly, but Gram is a slow eater, so we had to wait for her to finish her meal. Aunt Teen kept telling us to let Gram eat in peace, to stop rushing her. It felt like we had to wait a long time before Gram was ready to move into the living room.

Grace Bustill

Once we all got settled Gram said, "Tonight, I am going to start with Grace Bustill, the youngest Bustill child.

Grace Bustill opened a Quaker millinery store next to her father's bakery. She made custom hats for Quaker women. It was the custom of Quaker women to cover their heads with bonnets, and Grace made those bonnets. Grace, like her parents, lived a Quaker lifestyle, and she attended the Arch Street Quaker Meeting. She raised her children as Quakers, but her husband, Robert Douglas, was the minister and a founding member of the First African Presbyterian Church of Philadelphia."

Alex asked, "Is that the church you took us to last month? Is that Aunt Marion's church?"

Gram said, "Yes, it is. I wanted you to attend this church because our family was among the first members in 1807. Think about how long ago that was."

All of us kids said, "Wow!"

Gram continued by saying that Grace, like her father, started a school for children of color in her home. She co-founded the school with James Forten, a wealthy African-American sailmaker and a family friend. They wanted to ensure that their children and formerly enslaved children received an excellent education. Grace was active among female abolitionists in Philadelphia.

"Does anyone remember what an abolitionist was?"

Kevin raised his hand and said that abolitionists worked to end slavery and helped run-away slaves reach freedom. Gram smiled at him with pride.

Gram said, "Excellent, Kevin." Then she explained that Grace was a founding member of the Philadelphia Female Anti-Slavery Society and served as Vice President of the Convention of Women held in New York in 1837 and Philadelphia in 1838. She also worked for women to have the right to vote. Grace had six children. One of her sons, Robert Douglas, Jr., was a portrait artist, a sign painter, and an art teacher. He was a student of Thomas Sully, a very famous American portrait artist at the Pennsylvania Academy of Fine Arts, which rarely admitted "Negro" students. He also trained at the Royal Academy of Arts, while he was visiting London. Robert was asked to paint Queen Victoria's portrait. This was a huge honor. Unfortunately, the Secretary of State refused him a passport, saying he was "not a citizen." People of African descent were not granted "citizenship" until the Thirteenth Amendment of the United States Constitution passed the Congress in January 1865 and was ratified on December 6, 1865. Robert taught at the Institute for Colored Youth, now Cheyney University. He was also Philadelphia's first African-American photographer.

Gram told us that Grace's daughter, Sarah Mapps Douglass, was also a teacher and an artist. Among other things, she painted flowers. Gram had one of her paintings to show us.

Flower painted by Sarah Maps Douglas

"Sarah Mapps Douglass was educated by private tutors until 1819 when she attended an independent school in Philadelphia established by her mother and a family friend, James Forten. She later enrolled for classes at Pennsylvania Medical University. Women of color rarely attended this university. She used this training to teach health to her students. Sarah was an activist, abolitionist, and an artist. However, she was best known as a teacher who taught school for over thirty years. For many years, she taught at the Institute of Colored Youth and was responsible for the education of the girl students.

As you know, the Institute of Colored Youth became Cheyney University. Several members of our family graduated from Cheyney University. Sarah, like her grandparents and mother, adopted the lifestyle of the Society of Friends and devoted her life to the principles by which Quakers live. Although many members of our family adopted the Quaker lifestyle, the Bustill family was never accepted for membership because of the color of their skin. While white Quakers denounced slavery, and many were active abolitionists, they practiced segregation in their religious services. The Quakers established separate seating for people of color. Therefore, the Bustill family was forced to sit in the back of the meeting room on the "Colored Bench."

David Bustill

David Bustill, the youngest Bustill son, was also an abolitionist. David wrote that he felt that God had called him to help free enslaved people. He and his sons worked diligently to accomplish his goal. David worked as a plasterer, married Mary W Hicks, and they had a daughter and three sons. Like their father; Charles Hicks, James Mapps, and Joseph Cassey, were very active in the Underground Railroad.

Miles asked, "Gram, what type of railroad goes underground?"

Gram explained that the Underground Railroad is the name given to a secret network of routes and safe houses set up to help enslaved Africans escape to free states and Canada. The run-away slaves were not on a train. They were escaping from slavery by running through open fields, wooded areas, and along riverbeds. Men called "Slave Catchers" were paid to hunt them down and return the run-away slaves to their owners. It is said that the Underground Railroad got its name because, at a point, the Slave Catchers could not find the run-away slaves they were tracking. This was because abolitionists, like David and his sons, helped them hide or moved them to safer locations. When the Slave Catchers could not find the slaves, they declared that it was as if the slaves disappeared. They said there must be an underground railroad somewhere, taking them to freedom.

Elizabeth Bustill was David's only daughter. She became a teacher. For a short time, she was a student at the elite Centerburg Female Boarding School in Connecticut. When the school enrolled girls of color, the residents of the town closed down the school rather than have their daughters attend an integrated school. On May 24, 1833, the General Assembly enacted the "Black Law," making it illegal for out-of-state "Negro" students to attend a Connecticut school without local permission. On August 23, 1833, Prudence Crandall, the white headmistress of Centerburg, was arrested for violating the Black Law. Her first trial ended with the jury not able to reach a verdict because the Black Law was said to be unconstitutional. She was found guilty at her second trial when the judge declared that Negros were not citizens and not guaranteed rights under constitutional law. At her third trial, the guilty verdict was reversed because there was not enough information to convict her. To protect the students, the school was closed, and the girls sent home. Elizabeth completed her education at the Institute for Colored Youth in Philadelphia, Pennsylvania.

In the late 1850s, Joseph Cassey Bustill was a teacher living on Cranberry Street in Harrisburg, Pennsylvania. He worked with William Still as an agent of the Underground Railroad, moving run-away slaves from town to town on their way north to freedom. At only seventeen years old when he joined the Underground Railroad, he was reportedly the youngest agent.

Gram said, "I have copies of letters written by Joseph Bustill to Mr. Still about passengers on the Underground Railroad. Because men were looking for run-away slaves to return them to their owners, the Underground Railroad agents used coded language to protect the passengers. In one letter, Joseph told Mr. Still he put five large and three small packages on the road to Philadelphia from Harrisburg. He was telling Mr. Still that he put five adults and three children on the road to freedom. It is recorded that Joseph helped over a thousand run-away slaves to freedom during his lifetime. Joseph returned to Philadelphia after the Civil War and later relocated to Lincoln University, Pennsylvania, where he operated an inn.

Letter to Mr. William Still from Joseph C. Bustill

Harrisburg, March 24, 1856

Friend Still:

I suppose you have seen those five large and three small packages I sent by way of Reading, consisting of three men and women and children. They arrived here this morning at 8:30 [am] o'clock and left twenty minutes past three [pm]. You will please send me any information likely to prove interesting in relation to them. Lately, we have formed a society here called the Fugitive Slave Society. This is our first case, and I hope it will prove entirely successful. When you write, please inform me what signs or symbol you make use of in your dispatches, and any other information in relation to operations of the UR. Our reason for sending by the Reading Road, was to gain time; it is expected the owners will be in town this afternoon and by this Road we gained five hours' time, which is a matter of much importance, and we may have occasion to use it sometime in future. In great haste.

Yours with great respect, Joseph C. Bustill

Joseph and his wife had one child, Anna Bustill. She devoted much of her life to recording our family history, including several articles in the Journal of Negro History. Anna married James Humphrey Smith. She is known as the first Black genealogist in the United States. Because of her diligent work in collecting and recording the history of our family, we have the information I am sharing with you. She wrote *"The Bustill Family" in the Journal of Negro History.* At a time in this country's history when women did not have a profession or have their work published, Anna Bustill Smith published several books.

James Mapps Bustill worked with his brother, Charles, in their plastering business. Like his father and brothers, James was an outspoken abolitionist and a leader of his community. He was a member of several associations to extend the right to vote to all."

Gram looked up from her notes and said, "As free people of color, it was our responsibility to help others who were enslaved. Freedom for all was our family motto, that is why so many family members were active in the Underground Railroad.

Charles Hicks Bustill worked with his brother, James. Like his brothers, he was an abolitionist and a conductor on the Underground Railroad. Charles was one of the founding members of the Philadelphia Vigilance Committee. This group worked to assist run-away slaves. Despite the fact that Charles' wife died young, leaving him to raise his two daughters—Maria Louise and Gertrude—as a single dad, he devoted much of his time to helping run-away slaves.

Educating children was, and still is, very important in this family, so Charles enrolled his daughters in the Institute for Colored Youth. Both of his daughters became teachers. One of his daughters, Maria Louise Bustill, married Rev. William Drew Robeson, an escaped slave from North Carolina after he obtained his undergraduate and theology degrees at Lincoln University. Lincoln University is one of the oldest educational institutes for men of color in this country. The Robesons had five children: Benjamin became a pastor; William Jr. became a doctor; Reeve passed away young; Marian taught school in Philadelphia for over twenty years, and Paul was an actor, concert signer, and a human rights champion. Maria Louise died when Paul was six years old when her dress caught on fire while cooking."

Paul LeRoy Robeson

Gram asked if we remembered her telling us about cousin Paul? She said, "Paul LeRoy Robeson was a professional football player, a lawyer with a degree from Columbia University, an actor, a concert singer, and an activist, as well as a man of the people. He was respected around the world. As a student at Rutgers University, he was a five-letter man, which means he excelled in five sports. He was so smart that he was inducted into the honor society, Phi Beta Kapa, and was valedictorian of his graduating class. He was a political activist and traveled the globe, helping people in need and supporting human rights campaigns. In the 1950s, U.S. Senator Joseph McCarthy accused Paul of being a member of the Communist Party, and the U.S. State Department canceled his passport. Paul was 'blacklisted,' which means the government declared him disloyal to America. During this time, he was unable to get work in the United States, and without a passport, he could not leave the country to work. With these restrictions, Paul came up with a creative way to showcase his talents. He once stood in the middle of a bridge between Canada and the United States to sing. He performed for a Welsh festival using the transatlantic telephone connection. From 1951 to 1955, Paul published a newspaper, *Freedom*, that addressed issues of racism, colonialism, and human rights. You children should be very proud of the life Paul lived."

Gram said, "Charles Hicks Bustill's other daughter, Gertrude Emily Hicks Bustill, was a journalist, an author, a teacher, an activist, and a suffragette—someone who fought for women to have the right to vote. At a time when married women did not work outside the house, Gertrude wrote articles for many colored newspapers and served as the women's editor of the *New York Age* newspaper from 1885 to 1889. Gertrude married Nathan Mossell, the first African-American to graduate from the University of Pennsylvania School of Medicine. Nathan and Gertrude founded the first hospital for African-Americans in Philadelphia—the Fredrick Douglass Memorial Hospital and Training School. The hospital cared for sick African-Americans, provided opportunities for black physicians to work in the medical profession, and trained African-American nurses."

Gertrude Bustill Mossell Pennsylvania Historic Marker located at 1423 Lombard Street

(used with permission of the Pennsylvania Historical and Museum Commission)

Leah Bustill

"Our line of the Bustill family starts with Leah Bustill." said Gram, "She married Anthony Miller, and they had three children: Cyrus Bustill Miller, Elizabeth, and Rachel. Rachel was always sickly and died young. We are direct descendants of Leah and her son, Cyrus Bustill Miller. Cyrus Bustill Miller was a leader in his community. He was a member of several anti-slavery organizations and was an agent on the Underground Railroad. He recruited men for the United States Colored Troops (USCT) to fight in the Civil War. His son, Cyrus Bustill Miller, Jr., enlisted in the USCT, along with at least fourteen of his cousins. He was also a leader in his community.

Elizabeth Bustill Miller and her husband, Jacob C. White, Sr, were also leaders in the black community. They were business owners and philanthropists—which means they donated large sums of money to support free and enslaved people in their community. Jacob C White, Sr. was a rich man for his time. He owned many properties, including a burial ground—Lebanon Cemetery—where people of color were buried with dignity.

Chapel at Lebanon Cemetery - opened in 1849 and closed in 1903.

The cemetery was located at what is now the corner of 19th Street and Snyder Avenue in South Philadelphia. The Lebanon Cemetery office was a meeting site for local abolitionists and a distribution point for anti-slavery newspapers. The cemetery itself became a station stop on the Underground Railroad. To protect the Underground Railroad records, William Still secured his ledgers in the rafters of the Lebanon Cemetery chapel. When Lebanon closed, the bodies were dug up and reburied at historic Eden Cemetery.'"

Kevin said, "I know Eden Cemetery. Many famous African-Americans like Marian Anderson, Rev. Charles Albert Tindley, and William Still are buried there as well as lots of our family members. I remember going to Aunt Lillian's funeral at Eden Cemetery in Springfield, PA."

Gram continued our lesson by telling us that Jacob and Elizabeth's three sons enlisted in the United States Colored Troops (USCT) and trained at Camp William Penn. From 1863 to 1865, this camp trained colored troops who enlisted in the Union Army. Men of color could not become soldiers and sailors until after President Abraham Lincoln signed a proclamation permitting them to join the Union Army. The fourteen members of our family who enlisted in the United States Union Army all trained at Camp William Penn located in LaMott, Cheltenham Township, Pennsylvania. Today, a Civil War museum is located on the grounds of Camp William Penn.

Recruiting Poster
Camp William Penn located in LaMott, Cheltenham Township, Pennsylvania

Gram looked at her watch and said, "Well, children, I am sad to say that our family reunion weekend is ending, and some of you have a long trip home tomorrow. I think this is a good place to stop. You have learned about the beginning of our family here on this land and the contributions our family made from colonial days to the Civil War. When we are back together for Thanksgiving, we will continue our history lesson. Meanwhile, I want all of you to 'Go Forward and Be Great.'"

AJ said, "As long as I can remember, you've told us to 'Go Forward and Be Great,' now I understand are family motto. Thank you, Gram. I am so proud to be a member of this family."

I said, "We were born into an awesome family. Thank you, Gram, for the gift of our family history."

1912 Bustill Family Reunion Maple Shade Park Philadelphia, Pennsylvania

To my Family:

I wrote this book for you and for generations to come. My grandmother, Marion Abrams Miller lovingly known as Mimi, asked me to document our family history. I was able to trace our history in this country to Humphrey Morrey, the first mayor of Philadelphia, who arrived in New York in the 1670s; to Samuel Bustill, Deputy Registrar of the Colonial Province of West New Jersey in 1700s. You need to know your history to plan your future. So, "Go Forward and Be Great."

Thank you to everyone who provided input, including my siblings: Yvonne Wilmore, Morris Mosley, and Michael Mosley, and to Sala Wyman and Gwen Anthony. A special thank you to Adrian James; Girl Scout Troop 749 of Zion Baptist Church of Ardmore, Pennsylvania; and Jelani, Jasmine, and Jaliyah Taylor.

This book is dedicated to Dolores Miller Robinson, my mother, my role model, and my Shero.

2018 Bustill-Miller Family Reunion -- Five generations of Bustill\Miller Descendants